ESSENTIAL ELEMENTS

GUITAR ENSEMBLES

POP HITS

T0081968

CONTENTS

Arrangements by Tom Huizinga

ISBN 978-1-4234-2989-0

HAL•LEONARD®
CORPORATION
7777 W. BLUEMOUND RD. P.O. BOX 13819 MILWAUKEE, WI 53213

Visit Hal Leonard Online at
www.halleonard.com

BEST OF MY LOVE

Words and Music by John David Souther, Don Henley and Glenn Frey

BROWN EYED GIRL

Words and Music by Van Morrison

DREAMS

Words and Music by Stevie Nicks

DUST IN THE WIND

Words and Music by Kerry Livgren

EVERY BREATH YOU TAKE

Music and Lyrics by Sting

I GET AROUND

Words and Music by Brian Wilson and Mike Love

*Strum muted strings.

IMAGINE

Words and Music by John Lennon

Intro
Moderately slow

let ring throughout

Verse

*E♯ is played the same as F♮.

LET IT BE

Words and Music by John Lennon and Paul McCartney

MY CHERIE AMOUR

Words and Music by Stevie Wonder, Sylvia Moy and Henry Cosby

OH, PRETTY WOMAN

Words and Music by Roy Orbison and Bill Dees

STAND BY ME

Words and Music by Jerry Leiber, Mike Stoller and Ben E. King

*Pick muted string.

STILL THE SAME

Words and Music by Bob Seger

WONDERFUL TONIGHT

Words and Music by Eric Clapton

Y.M.C.A.

Words and Music by Jacques Morali, Henri Belolo and Victor Willis

YOUR SONG

Words and Music by Elton John and Bernie Taupin

ESSENTIAL ELEMENTS FOR GUITAR

Essential Elements Comprehensive Guitar Method

Take your guitar teaching to a new level! With popular songs in a variety of styles, and quality demonstration and backing tracks on the accompanying online audio, *Essential Elements for Guitar* is a staple of guitar teachers' instruction – and helps beginning guitar students off to a great start. This method was designed to meet the National Standards for Music Education, with features such as cross-curricular activities, quizzes, multicultural songs, basic improvisation and more.

BOOK 1
INCLUDES TAB
by Will Schmid and Bob Morris

Concepts covered in Book 1 include: getting started; basic music theory; guitar chords; notes on each string; music history; ensemble playing; performance spotlights; and much more! Songs include: Dust in the Wind • Eleanor Rigby • Every Breath You Take • Hey Jude • Hound Dog • Let It Be • Ode to Joy • Rock Around the Clock • Stand by Me • • Sweet Home Chicago • This Land Is Your Land • You Really Got Me • more!

00862639 Book/Online Audio $17.99
00001173 Book Only $10.99

BOOK 2
by Bob Morris

Concepts taught in Book 2 include: playing melodically in positions up the neck; movable chord shapes up the neck; scales and extended chords in different keys; fingerpicking and pick style; improvisation in positions up the neck; and more! Songs include: Auld Lang Syne • Crazy Train • Folsom Prison Blues • La Bamba • Landslide • Nutcracker Suite • Sweet Home Alabama • Your Song • and more.

00865010 Book/Online Audio $17.99
00120873 Book Only $10.99

Essential Elements Guitar Ensembles

The songs in the Essential Elements Guitar Ensemble series are playable by three or more guitars. Each arrangement features the melody, a harmony part, and bass line in standard notation along with chord symbols. For groups with more than three or four guitars, the parts can be doubled. This series is perfect for classroom guitar ensembles or other group guitar settings.

Essential Elements Guitar Songs
INCLUDES TAB

The **[ ]** books in the Essential Elements Guitar Songs series feature popular songs selected for the practice of specific guitar chord types. Each book includes eight songs and a CD with fantastic sounding play-along tracks. Practice at any tempo with the included Amazing Slow Downer software!

BARRE CHORD ROCK
00001137 Late-Beginner Level $12.99

POWER CHORD ROCK
00001139 Mid-Beginner Level $15.99

More Resources

Mid-Beginner Level

EASY POP SONGS
00865011/$10.99

CHRISTMAS CLASSICS
00865015/$9.99

CHRISTMAS SONGS
00001136/$10.99

Late Beginner Level

CLASSICAL THEMES
00865005/$9.99

POP HITS
00001128/$10.99

ROCK CLASSICS
00865001/$9.99

TURBO ROCK
00001076/$9.95

Early Intermediate Level

J.S. BACH
00123103/$9.99

THE BEATLES
00172237/$9.99

CHRISTMAS FAVORITES
00128600/$9.99

DISNEY SONGS
00865014/$12.99

IRISH JIGS & REELS
00131525/$9.99

JAZZ BALLADS
00865002/$9.99

MULTICULTURAL SONGS
00160142/$9.99

POPULAR SONGS
00241053/$9.99

TOP SONGS 2010-2019
00295218/$9.99

Mid-Intermediate Level

THE BEATLES
00865008/$14.99

BLUES CRUISE
00000470/$9.95

BOSSA NOVA
00865006/$12.99

CHRISTMAS CLASSICS
00865015/$9.99

DUKE ELLINGTON
00865009/$9.99

GREAT THEMES
00865012/$10.99

JIMI HENDRIX
00865013/$9.99

JAZZ STANDARDS
00865007/$12.99

MYSTERIOSO
00000471/$9.95

ROCK HITS
00865017/$9.99

ROCK INSTRUMENTALS
00123102/$9.99

TOP HITS
00130606/$9.99

Late Intermediate to Advanced Level

JAZZ CLASSICS
00865016/$9.99

DAILY GUITAR WARM-UPS
by Tom Kolb
Mid-Beginner to Late Intermediate
00865004 Book/Online Audio $14.99

GUITAR FLASH CARDS
96 Cards for Beginning Guitar
00865000... $10.99

Prices, contents, and availability subject to change without notice.

HAL•LEONARD®
www.halleonard.com

0621
404